T0304356

DO US A FAVOR

Do Us a Favor

Copyright © 2021 by Kevin Risner

All rights reserved. No part of this book may
be reproduced, scanned, or distributed in any
printed or electronic form without permission.

Published in the United States of America

Published by Variant Literature Inc

Cover design by Olivia Croom Hammerman
www.ochbookdesign.com

Table of Contents

To those who have ever felt insignificant, have considered their words or beliefs or something else about themselves as not worthy, you ARE. More than worthy.

To my friends who may be struggling
To my wife who read (and loved) this first
To my family members that have supported me
And to anyone reading this: THANK YOU.

We got five years

… oh, what a surprise!

+

David Bowie's a prophet.

The five-year countdown started early on in 2016 when he flew back to Mars. Then, that June, the Cavaliers won an NBA Championship. We should have been on the alert when that happened. We should've known we'd been bumped off the proper timeline.

We left
        Cleveland
                on a belated honey-moon trip to Canada. The Republican National Convention barreled through two days after we left. We'd escaped! We meandered the streets of Montreal instead. Eyes on sky. Eyes on summer. One night, I ate duck. She ate filet. We shared a bottle of white wine. Next afternoon, we climbed Mont Royal. Inched closer and closer to Nova Scotia.

We sank into beach chairs in the afternoon of one of the hottest Julys in the province's history. We should have stayed, dug our feet in the sand, planted them so we could blast off into the sky. No need for jetpacks.

+

You know what's wild: We really would have met the Starman up there. He'd have blown our minds as he belted every word out through open space, orbiting phrases like:

> *I'm an alligator*
> *I'm a mama-papa coming for you*
> *I'm the space invader*
> *I'll be a rock 'n rollin' bitch for you*

+

We'd reach the perfect locale, in due time, where the Spiders from Mars would still pitch stakes in our souls. They'd be hosting an end-of-the-world party.

I think we'd lose it there: to see them all together again, to see us all in one place, sun struck
  sun stuck in our eyes, see ourselves swimming in the champagne of lost galaxies
    floating and remembering every single thing about this godforsaken world.

+

The rest is just a blip in the here and now

  and now
    even now
    gimme your hands
      gimme them!

'cause you're wonderful!
    and *you're not alone!*

Gimme your hands
    and we'll be the brightest we've ever been.

With lyrics from three songs on David Bowie's perfect album
    The Rise and Fall of Ziggy Stardust and the Spiders from Mars:
    "FiveYears," "Moonage Daydream," and "Rock'n Roll Suicide."

I had an

opportunity to learn from you

it is true   these were unique

elections

When running

four miles on the towpath trail, conversation is often at a premium. There's gravel crunching underfoot. It rains. The ground sinks. Puddles lake on the edges. Rain hasn't touched the rest of the world in weeks. Only here. Always only here. It's one of the cooler evenings at the end of summer. Gnats have not arrived yet. Glasses should protect us from the attack. We mention the border wall. My friend shouts it's all bullshit. *His supporters think they're animals,* he says. And then—*We're all darker. We all look different than them. To them, we're not humans.* Our legs leap forward in tandem, our pulses in step, each crunch an affirmation. *People have called me Chinese,* he adds. But he doesn't use that term. Disgust hangs in the air, at the ignorance that surrounds us, at the ignorance that has simmered for decades. *To them, we're all the same. Look at one person, and they look like the next.* There is no surprise at these statements anymore. There's no surprise about November in Ohio. There's no surprise at what we see phone-recorded, shared online. The words we see on screens, on walls, on skin. There's always another mile, another evening, another deep breath.

When I see my wife

eyed suspiciously by an agent at the airport because of her last name, I want to speak up and yell back: *do you really think she has something in her shoe to detonate when we're high in the air?* But I say nothing, we stand and wait, we blister with anger.

A name from somewhere over

there

elicits fear, some dormant poison set to ruin one's life. The watchdogs bark, saliva splatters in all directions because the tiniest of mice have darted into view.

I want to say something in this TSA line I'm going to say something this time I'm truly going to I'm *going* to I *am*—

But I say nothing—

We open our pockets take off shoes plop belts onto the conveyor belt flash our laptops for all to see allow others to roll their hands up and down our bodies *just in case just in case just in* fucking *case.*

I would like you to do us a favor though

surround   yourself with
the same people

nonsense ended

a lot of it started
Whatever you   do, it's   important   you do it

ready to open a new page

Press hand

against the pane / peek below / ocean sinks into shoreline sand / imagine feet sticking inside and tunneling for cool pockets / hiding like clams in noontime heat / to soar means to ingest the chill of the stratosphere / the boundary between oneself and ice crystals in the sky / a pinprick thousands of feet away from solidity / knowing how small one really is is a revelation in these ascending minutes / boxed in with metal all around / upon descent the view becomes a shroud / the jolts remind me nothing's ever certain / the climb toward maturity feels identical / as a seven-year-old one thinks those at a higher age are all-knowing / at 30 and beyond I laugh / at those snapshots of the '90s / I do not wonder anymore about the future / about wisdom / about much of anything anymore

With the bedsheets wrapped around me

I'm the best-in-the-city burrito / ravenous at one a.m. / I make a jaunt to the refrigerator / receive a revelation of string cheese / I never know when I am almost asleep / minnows dart underneath rippling currents / these fish nibble at my feet / events not worthy of repetition most radiator midnights / I turn to the rain-streaked window / where winds rush and rattle the glass / I imagine this space / this rectangular cut-out of existence / as holy / I pray to the great overhead / hear the choir around me / I jump to the 90th floor / far from concrete and gum stains / no more stepping on the pink with new Nikes / I want to live in this space / an aerie protected from the tentacles of the deep / from swooping predators / from forks of electricity slicing a pathway to infinitude / I'm a dot amidst a collection of dots / billions and billions of dots alive and breathing / one of trillions and trillions of consciousnesses / here or in the past or in the ether of eternity / I picture where I exist / a constellation / neighbors to Cancer and Leo / wedged in the middle / both ends on the attack / I wonder how I'm able to be / when there's no reason / to be no more

I   wanted to assure you

we are friends

You smiled at each person entering your cafe

dice in your hands to start backgammon beneath lights that hide identities of couples huddled in corners. You practiced your English phrases tinged with Turkish, superficial twists catching in the smoke. Other people chatted after daylight had faded, a party passing around the nargile pipe, inhaling rose and mint. You never mentioned your ancestry to me, but I'd heard about it from a friend after you left to farm in a distant part of the country. I wondered why. And then I recalled what people think and say when they hear the word Kurdish—

evil, terrorists, barbarians, baby-killers

—without a pause. The dissonance stains walls, on names, on certain groups of people. The thought burns me, pumps fire into my body where only blood used to pulse thick and constant. There are those who will keep climbing the stairs into the café, purchase tea and pucker lips on mouth-pieces. They won't pucker at the friction. They will obscure their visions of others. They will sit behind a curtain, not pulled back until much later in life, perhaps when some become more comfortable with each other, but not enough to whisper secrets that could now get one killed.

The back wall has always been empty

The back wall has always been empty—angry. There is no door, no tapestries, no portraits. Not even etchings or lines or notches in the stone. Sweat drips down my face even without physical exertion. Hands pass over chilled stone as if there's a section that's an entrance into another world. Who enters through the wall? Who would? And how long ago? A cloaked figure—faceless with outstretched hands shaking—reaches out toward it, hums words I cannot decipher. After the incantation, the wall flashes. The vibrations turn palpable. Even if I do not come into contact with this wall, anything can reach me as I sit on the sofa in that room.

+

The back wall has always been empty—open. Coals glow constantly, no matter what. Even when they're the dimmest they've ever been. A collection of orbs. Each one invites me to jump into them, soar through time. See snapshots of walks down cobblestoned alleyways, planes curving over seas, memories tinged sepia. When I whisper, my voice floats like a sneeze's afterthought. What new city, what new country, what new world is on the other side? The smell of strawberries, the tops sliced off. The sandbar's blinding reflection, turtles trudging for the waves. A blanket of heat from the nearest bonfire.

+

The back wall has always been empty—ready. Back in that room. I recline, hold the mouthpiece, hope lemons find a space inside my chest, scratch ink along the lined paper of my notebook, save everything that was once forgotten. This heavy weather turns into a portal. Winds glide with the cold front, snow drifts against doorways, cars careen into one another, lights pop off, the portal blinks to signal its closure. I hold tight and steadfast until the time comes for it to open again.

Make a left down the alley

In the winter there's an orange glow at seven p.m. Glistening charcoal like beating hearts. Vibrant and alive. There's a canopy stretching over and down windows to protect occupants from the sea spray. The front door is a flap of plastic. Enter without thinking and the warmth hits you. Indistinct visions appear. Chatter grows viscous like noon haze.

In the summer during the most humid ten p.m. It feels like a boxing-glove fist. When upstairs alone in self-made smoke I notice the balcony rail untouched by human hands. The smoke collects sound. Car horns and yowling cats and remnants of conversations from elders. A starless heaviness presses against everything alive. Like the bottommost floor after an earthquake.

Midnight muffles the cries for help.

A lot of people are talking

On a bike

on a path in the woods / it rained yesterday and this morning / mud sprays all around like the spotted redness of horror films especially when I twist the handlebars / curve the back wheel around a sharp turn / as humans we spray everything / marking each thing as ours / every object / this tree that path this person that philosophy / if it isn't ours yet it will be soon / if others follow my lead on this path they will undoubtedly find me / even if I try to hide they will tread over the same tracks / even after a dry spell the treads are the most natural pattern we know

If there is no more electricity

do this / before the final surge comes print out my words / press every line onto my tongue / stamp the ink there / the paper will disintegrate / I'll swirl it around like an oaky Shiraz and ingest the pages I have left / each letter and diacritic will remain a part of me / for years and years / until my cells replenish / I'll construct an encyclopedia / much larger than my initial meal of words and phrases and paragraphs and chapters / this is only a preventative measure / to consume everything before the powers that be / bring torches and ignite what's left / to savor the sweetness each character holds / before the ink sinks into ash / soon to nothing / flames lick the pulp and splinters of fallen earthen beauty / make these words brighter than any bonfire / brighter than the sun / ballooning into the world / setting off sprinkler systems

Tonight is the night to look at the sky

find targets / meteors zip into deepest black / act as laser pointers / I want to pounce on them / I never catch them in time / a new life appears / soon it's gone out of existence / much like mayflies along the lake rest on white walls of houses one morning / then crunched underfoot in the darkness later that evening / I shake more when I sit still / breath pours out onto polished surfaces / my whole self wipes blank during the endless winter months / when Betelgeuse explodes in the sky it will have already been gone for ages / I am under covers / embroidered / eyes wide open / seeing nothing and everything all at once / matter in front of me morphs into flickering flame / touches my tongue so I can say what no one understands / another language whispers goodnight in this not-so-distant space / warmth spreads through my veins / comets are not ice any longer / but indestructible fire

                                        restore   honesty

                                                       if you have
                    information   it would
be very helpful   to make sure we
administer justice

.

My eyes boggle

at the complacency of the world. We are all lottery balls inside see-through containers. Push a button. I'll get sucked up through a hyper-speed vacuum tube. If only we all could travel in the same way: in vessels like the ones you put deposit slips in! Race from where we sit all the way to the bank. We've been quarantining ourselves for what seems like eternity. Until eternity ceases to exist. How special, to bask in solitude until the solitude swells beyond containment! I see what I want to see. I shrug off the rest. Like a robe before showering. Like the leaves you've sprinkled over me in a fit of playfulness. If I leave my eyes open too long, they swell redder than a heart. In that space, that's where we keep the most vulnerable. How long did we let everything slide away until dystopia became our present reality? Perhaps it was when we saw the worst possible thing. When we tilted our heads back and gasped, as many times as we could, with our final store of oxygen, and then shouted in our loudest of loud voices:

OK! OK! OK!

You win.

Three borders

Rectangle front lawns with flamingos
Cake tin molds
Always envious of the adjacent box
Of the other's most recent thing

If I stepped off the sidewalk onto the grass
Each morning before sunrise
The dew would stick to my shoes
Even after I walked back home

The proper alignment in our lives is never right
An endless hangnail
Pull the skin away
How much of us can stay alive when full
-y separated

thank you for your invitation

Two faiths

cross >> wooden, hand-cut, giver unknown, full of rekindled proclamations of faiths hidden, unseen in a drawer full of matchbox cars and staples, floppy disks and highlighters. Twenty-five years whirl in a velodrome, bikes without brakes, round and round and round, no end in sight. At age thirty-six, I use the same track, a scarf to cover my eyes, paint over massacres on TVs, on each new browser, each contraption, each contraction, each breath.

prayer beads >> forest-green, reminds others of a rosary, a present from my first landlord in Istanbul as we parted ways, a talisman. Once in late November he, his wife, a colleague, and I ate hamsi together, fishes fried whole, lemon and onion and parsley on the side. After the meal there was Turkish coffee. I couldn't refrain. I was afraid of sleeping past the alarm for next day's classes. But I woke up in time.

You had your soul with you

mine hung on the flagpole / when the temperature reached 90 degrees for
three days straight / again / *you have no idea how hard I died when you left* / the
back seat is lined with towels / dried leaves on the floor / towers of library
books I haven't read / never will / where do passengers go for respite / a
seat at the bar with a beer and a glass / to inspect the counter for hidden
grime / there's always a recounting of the past decade / a lazy day parade /
a sham election / *I was in no mood* to hear this / strings of lyrics pausing in
the sky / wait for change that won't come / I am *carried to space by a dolphin
balloon* / there's a voice snaking in the silence right before sleep / in the pain
in the middle of a fork in the road / at a wrong turn / there's heartbreaking
truth in the raspiest of voices / love submerged with an underwater chorus
/ vibrating light emanates from our chests / I gasp as this one song pauses
at the bridge / it crawls and peeks over the edge into the river / maybe
souls can be moved / *here … at the end of everything*

With lyrics from two songs on The National's most recent album *I Am
Easy to Find*: "You Had Your Soul with You" and "The Pull of You".

The whole world was
upset

Hibernation sounds like paradise

when you have been awake for a whole week, eyes glued to the news, ears pinned to the walls

Can you just wait here with me?

a vat of honey is what we dive into, we'll stick around for the long haul, mosquitos in amber, people on rafts float above us on the surface, square-shaped silhouettes beneath the sun

Can you describe them for me?

each fuzzy guitar rockets me back to the late '90s, when band members would stare at their feet, the lead singer shouting as loud as they could to share some intangible passion to the lost ones staring at the ceiling

Can you just wait here with me?

everything's a mess, all I want to hear are the voices of my friends, if I heard the voices of those I thought I'd never hear again in my dreams, I'd never *ever* want to wake up

With lyrics from "Describe" on Perfect Genius's most recent album: *Set My Heart On Fire Immediately.*

Afterword

In early December of 2019, I was falling into a rabbit hole of news stories and NPR coverage on the impeachment hearings. With constant references to the phone call between Donald Trump and Volodymyr Zelenskyy during the proceedings, I was pulled to read the transcript in its entirety. I had only read excerpts, but I needed the full picture of the conversation. As I was reading, I highlighted phrases and statements that stood out to me. It was then, as I was exploring this transcript, that I wanted to collect some of these statements and merge them into an erasure poem. I'd been inspired earlier that year by various erasures, most notably Tracy K. Smith's "Declaration" while reading Wade in the Water. Smith's poem left me speechless, in awe. I felt compelled to explore this genre that December, craft another erasure, provide statements that looked innocuous when read independent of the Trump/Zelenskyy phone call—a conversation that was anything but innocuous. Furthermore, I wanted this poem to read less like a conversation and more a mix of declarations and axioms, the speaker unknown, adjacent and similar to the narrator throughout the chapbook. I made it a point not to share which individual said what things in the poem. Obviously, "I would like you to do us a favor though" is infamously impossible to remove from Trump's lips. The other statements, less so. I was struck by some of these phrases, and I wondered how they could be said by either individual, especially grouped as they were, most notably:

		restore	honesty
			if you have
	information		it would
be very helpful		to make sure	we
administer justice			

and "The whole world was / upset."

At the completion of this erasure poem and after its publication, along with Trump's initial impeachment in the House, I returned to this poem and had the urge to fracture it further. I deleted a few more words, and separated them into chunks. I interspersed other poems—some published others unpublished (and initially unwritten)—around them. With feverish edits and restructuring, I had a draft of this chapbook completed in March, right as the pandemic reached the United States and continued to wreak havoc all over the world. The poems themselves took a new shape, held a heavier weight, and possessed a different poignancy that hadn't existed mere weeks earlier. I believe these poems still resonate, some even more so, as we continue to confront the COVID-19 pandemic and bear the fallout of Trump's (and others') seditious exploits. As 2021 nears its conclusion and as we trudge through the great unknown of a post-Trump world, we can truly look at where we're at as a country and as a society and make the necessary changes to restore honesty, administer justice, and live in a world less upset and more whole.

Acknowledgements

Earlier versions of these poems, boasting different titles, can be found in the following books and journals:

"You smile at each person entering your café," "Make a left down the alley," and "Two faiths" in My Ear is a Sieve, originally published by Bottlecap Press, 2017.

"When I see my wife" in Rising Phoenix Review (2017).

"On a bike" in The Bookends Review (2018).

"You had your soul with you" in Perhappened Mag (2020).

Pages that have erased text are excerpts of the phone call conversation Donald Trump had with Ukrainian President Volodymyr Zelenskyy on July 25th, 2019. This erasure poem, as a whole, was published as "I Would Like You To Do Us a Favor..." as a part of Glass Poetry's Poets Resist series (2020).

About the Author

Kevin A. Risner is a product of Ohio. When he's not putting pen to paper, you can usually find him running on the trails or hiking with his wife Sunday mornings. His work has recently been published or is forthcoming in The Aurora Journal, Lucent Dreaming, The Ocean State Review, Moonchild Magazine, Perhappened Mag, Fahmidan Journal, and many others.